Appetizers/Beverages

ARMADILLO EGGS

These freeze so well, you may wish to double recipe.

Wash and drain .... 2 cans (11 oz. ea.) whole **MILD PICKLED JALAPENO PEPPERS**, devein and seed

Set aside. Grate .... 1 pound **CHEDDAR CHEESE**
Stuff **PEPPERS** and
  add rest of cheese to .... 1 pound regular **PORK SAUSAGE**
  1 1/2 cup **BISCUIT MIX**

Set aside. Beat well .... 2 **EGGS**

Set aside. Pat about 1 tablespoon sausage mixture in palm of hand. Lay pepper stuffed with cheese on sausage. Pat mixture around pepper. Seal dough real well so that cheese will not come out of pepper.

Dip in beaten **EGGS**; roll in ...... 1 package **PORK SHAKE AND BAKE**

Place on ungreased cookie sheet. Bake 30-40 minutes in preheated 350-degree oven.

 **HOT TIP**   *Always wear rubber gloves when working with peppers.*

JALAPENO RELLENOS

Always wear rubber gloves when working with peppers.

Rinse and drain .... 12 pickled **JALAPENO PEPPERS**
Slit one side, lengthwise, remove seeds and veins. Leave stems attached. Set aside.
Beat until fluffy .... 3 ounces **CREAM CHEESE**
Add... 1/2 cup **CHEDDAR CHEESE**, shredded
1/2 cup **GREEN ONION**, diced tops also

Stuff each pepper with cheese mixture. Place on baking sheet. Bake in preheated
350-degree oven about 10 minutes, or until cheese melts. Top each pepper with a
PIMENTO STRIP.

*QUICK APPETIZER: Brush large FLOUR TORTILLAS lightly with
melted BUTTER. Sprinkle with grated CHEESE. Broil until cheese melts,
and tortilla is crispy brown.*

▼ ▼ ▼ ▼ ▼ ▼ ▼ ▼ ▼ ▼ ▼ ▼ ▼ ▼ ▼ ▼ ▼ ▼ 7

NACHOS
NUMERO UNO!

Spread on baking sheet **TORTILLA CHIPS**, or **LARGE CORN CHIPS.** Sprinkle with shredded **CHEDDAR** or **MONTEREY JACK CHEESE**. Top with canned **GREEN CHILI PEPPERS** or **SLICED JALAPENO PEPPERS**. VARIATIONS: Cover chips with **REFRIED BEANS, COLBY CHEESE, SALSA**. Or, brown **LEAN GROUND BEEF** and **ONIONS**. Cover chips. Add **CHEESE, REFRIED BEANS**, sliced **JALAPENOS.**

DURANGO SPECIALTY
Hot smokies at their best.

Cut each triangle of **CRESCENT DOUGH** in half lengthwise. Will have 16 pieces. At widest end of dough, place 1 **COCKTAIL SAUSAGE**, 1 slice pickled **JALAPENO PEPPER**, and a slice of **CHEDDAR CHEESE**. Roll dough from widest end to narrow end. Place on greased cookie sheet. Bake in preheated 350-degree oven for 12 minutes or until brown. Serve with **PICA DE GALLO** or **PICANTE SAUCE**.

QUESADILLAS
May fry or bake in oven.

Have ready to use ....   1 package **FLOUR TORTILLAS**
           SHREDDED CHEDDAR CHEESE
           MILD PICANTE SAUCE or **TACO SAUCE**

TO FRY:
Place a layer of cheese over one-half of tortilla. Sprinkle with mild picante sauce. Fold over and fry each tortilla in hot **OIL** until crisp and brown on each side. Drain on paper towels.

TO BAKE:
Lay tortillas flat on cookie sheets. Place cheese and picante sauce on tortilla, leaving $1/2$ inch space around edge of tortilla. Place second tortilla on top. Broil tortillas until they begin to brown.

▼ ▼ ▼ ▼ ▼ ▼ ▼ ▼ ▼ ▼ ▼ ▼ ▼ ▼ ▼ ▼ ▼   9

DIPS OF THE WILD WEST
VARIATIONS of Con Queso dips.

BASIC CON QUESO:
Heat together ....   1 can (10 oz.) **CHOPPED TOMATOES** and
                                               GREEN CHILIES
                                             1 pound **VELVEETA CHEESE**, cubed

Serve with **CHIPS**.

WILD WEST VERSION:
Crumble, cook, and drain well 1 pound **HOT SAUSAGE** or 1 pound **GROUND MEAT.** Add to mix.

CHORIZO CON QUESO:
Crumble, cook and drain well $^1/_2$ pound **CHORIZO SAUSAGE**. Add to cheese. Add small jar canned **MUSHROOMS**, drained.

FIESTA TACO DIP

A great appetizer with a Mexican flair.

On large platter, spread	1 can (32 oz.) **REFRIED BEANS**
Cover with mixture of	3 ripe **AVOCADOS**, peel and mash
	1 **TOMATO**, diced
	1½ tsp. **LEMON JUICE**
	1½ tsp. **GARLIC POWDER**
	2 Tbsp. **ONION**, minced
	TABASCO to taste
	SALT and **PEPPER**
Cover with mixture of	1 cup **SOUR CREAM**
	1 cup **MAYONNAISE**
	1 package **TACO SEASONING**
Layer over mixture	4 **TOMATOES,** chopped
	1 bunch **GREEN ONIONS**, chopped
	8 ounces **CHEDDAR CHEESE**, grated
	1 can (4.5 oz.) **RIPE OLIVES**, chopped

Serve with **TOSTADOS.** VARIATION: Layer with 1 pound browned ground **BEEF**.

▼ ▼ ▼ ▼ ▼ ▼ ▼ ▼ ▼ ▼ ▼ ▼ ▼ ▼ ▼ ▼ ▼ 11

PANCHO'S HOT BROCCOLI DIP
Our favorite appetizer!!

Cook according to directions....	2 packages **FROZEN BROCCOLI**, chopped
Brown in small amount of **OIL**........................	1 pound **FRESH MUSHROOMS**, sliced
	1 **ONION**, chopped
	4 stalks **CELERY**, diced
Add...	1 can **CREAM MUSHROOM SOUP**
	12 ounces **GARLIC CHEESE**
	1 tsp. **LEMON**
	SALT and **PEPPER**

Add drained **BROCCOLI** and serve warm with **TORTILLA CHIPS.**

OLDIE but GOODIE: Simmer equal parts of PICANTE SAUCE and HONEY until thickened. Add cubes of cooked HAM, TURKEY, or COCKTAIL SAUSAGES. Serve with picks.

NINFA'S FAMOUS AVOCADO DIP

Ninfa's is one of the best Mexican food restaurants in the southwest.

Peel and mash..............................	2 ripe **AVOCADOS**
Add..	5 Tbsp. **LEMON JUICE**
	$^1/_2$ cup **SOUR CREAM**
	$^1/_2$ cup **MILK**
	3 tsp. minced **ONION**
Stir in	2 Tbsp. minced **FRESH CILANTRO** or
	$^1/_2$ tsp. **DRIED CILANTRO**
	1 tsp. **HOT PEPPER SAUCE**
	2 cloves **GARLIC**, pressed
	SALT

Mix together and refrigerate for at least 1 hour. Serve with **TORTILLA CHIPS**.

▼ ▼ ▼ ▼ ▼ ▼ ▼ ▼ ▼ ▼ ▼ ▼ ▼ ▼ ▼ ▼ ▼ ▼   13

SOUTHWEST DIP

A very mild dip.

Mix together ....
1 can (14 oz.) **TOMATOES**, chopped
1 can (4 oz.) **CHOPPED GREEN CHILIES**
1 can (4¹/₂ oz.) **CHOPPED BLACK OLIVES**
4 **GREEN ONIONS**, chopped
1¹/₂ tsp. **WHITE VINEGAR**
3 Tbsp. **OLIVE OIL**
1 tsp. each **SUGAR, GARLIC SALT, PEPPER**

For hotter dip add finely chopped **JALAPENO PEPPER**. Best if allowed to set a few hours before serving. Serve with **TORTILLA CHIPS**.

MARGARITA

Rub rim of glass with **LIME** wedge. Swirl in **MARGARITA SALT.** Combine in cocktail shaker, 2 oz. **TEQUILA**, ³/₄ oz. **TRIPLE SEC**, 1¹/₂ oz. **LIME** or **LEMON JUICE**, **ICE CUBES**. Shake vigorously, strain into salt-rimmed glass. 1 SERVING.

GUACAMOLE

Mexican avocado dip. Taste tested.

Mash .... 3 ripe **AVOCADOS**
Add and stir .... 1¹/₂ Tbsp. **LEMON JUICE**
Add .... 1 **TOMATO**, chopped
                                                     ¹/₂ **ONION**, chopped
                                                     1 cup **LETTUCE**, chopped
                                                     ¹/₄ cup **PICANTE**
Season to taste with .... **GARLIC SALT** and **PEPPER**

Serve with warm **CORN CHIPS**.

CAFÉ MEXICANO

Fill coffee mug with 1 oz. **KAHLUA**, ¹/₂ oz. **BRANDY**, 1 teaspoon **CHOCOLATE SYRUP**. Fill with **HOT COFFEE**. Top with **WHIPPED CREAM** and dash **CINNA-MON**. 1 SERVING.

TEJAS CHEESE DIP
A mild creamy, cheesy dip.

Melt in microwave	1 pound **VELVEETA CHEESE**, cubed
Add	8 ounces **CREAM CHEESE**
	1 pint **SALAD DRESSING**
	3 cloves **GARLIC**, minced
	2 ounces **PIMENTOS**, diced
	4 ounces **CHOPPED CHILIES**
	4 boiled **EGGS**, diced

Will keep well in refrigerator. Serve with **TORTILLA CHIPS**.

SOBER SANGRIA

In $2^1/_2$ qt. pitcher combine 2 cups **CRANBERRY JUICE**, 2 cups **ORANGE JUICE**, 2 tablespoons **LEMON JUICE**, 1 qt. **STRAWBERRY SODA**. Chill well. Add 1 **LIME**, **LEMON**, and **ORANGE**, sliced thin and serve over **ICE CUBES** in tall glasses. 14 - 16 SERVINGS.

ARMANDO'S GREEN SALSA

Chop in blender .... 1 **GARLIC** clove
6 **TOMATILLOS**, halved
2 **GREEN TOMATOES**, quartered

Pour mixture into skillet and cook 4 to 5 minutes. Return to blender.

Add and puree with .... 2 **JALAPENOS,** roasted, seeded
1 **AVOCADO**

Fold in .... 4 Tbsp. **SOUR CREAM**
SALT and **PEPPER**

Serve as a dip for **TOSTADOS** or as **SALSA.**

BLUE MARGARITAS

Moisten rims of Margarita glasses with lime. Invert into **MARGARITA SALT**. (Coarse salt.) Chill glasses. In blender, combine 6 ounces **TEQUILA**, 6 ounces **FROZEN LIMEADE** concentrate, 1/3 cup **BLUE CURACO**. Blend well. With blender running, add 3 cups **CRUSHED ICE**. Blend until slushy. Pour into chilled glasses. Garnish with **LIME SLICE**. 8 SERVINGS.

GOOOOOD HOT STUFF

Some like it HOT, some like it NOT! Adjust peppers.

Chop or dice .... 2 ripe **TOMATOES**
$^1/_2$ **ONION** red, if available
1 fresh **JALAPENO PEPPER**, remove seeds and membrane
Add to taste............................... **LEMON JUICE**
GARLIC SALT
SEASONED SALT (just a little)

Stir together. Refrigerate 1 hour. Serve with **TORTILLA CHIPS.**

SANGRIA

Cook over medium heat, 1 cup **ORANGE JUICE**, 1 cup **SUGAR**, until sugar is dissolved. Cool completely. Pour mixture into pitcher with 1 fifth **DRY RED WINE**, 2 oz. **BRANDY**, 1 **LIME**, **LEMON**, and **ORANGE**, sliced very thin. Refrigerate no longer than 1 hour. To serve, stir in 1 cup **CLUB SODA**. Pour over **ICE CUBES** in tall glasses. Garnish with **ORANGE SLICES**. 6 - 8 SERVINGS.

Breakfast/Brunch

HUEVOS RANCHEROS
Served traditionally with refried beans.

Heat in microwave to soften .....   6 (6-inch) **CORN TORTILLAS**

(May fry in hot **OIL**, 5 seconds on each side, or until softened.) Line a 13x9x2-inch baking dish with tortillas, letting tortillas extend $^1/_2$ inch up sides of dish. Set aside.

Brown in skillet ....   2 Tbsp. **oil**
                                  $^1/_2$ cup **ONION**, chopped
                                  1 **GARLIC** clove, minced

Add...   3 large **TOMATOES**, chopped
                                  1 can (4 oz.) **CHOPPED GREEN CHILIES**
                                  $^1/_4$ tsp. **SALT**

Simmer, uncovered, 10 minutes, stirring occasionally. Pour mixture over tortillas. Make 6 indentations in tomato mixture. Break an **EGG** into each. Cover and bake in preheated 350-degree oven for 25 minutes. Sprinkle with grated **CHEESE** and bake until cheese is melted. Serve immediately.

MEXICAN EGGS
"Migas".

Melt in a large skillet.................. 2 Tbsp. **MARGARINE**

Mix, pour into skillet
  and stir gently .... 6 **EGGS**

$^1/_2$ tsp. **TABASCO SAUCE**

$^1/_2$ **ONION**, chopped

$^1/_4$ **GREEN BELL PEPPER**, chopped

When almost cooked add .... 1 cup **CHEDDAR CHEESE**, grated

1 cup **TOSTADOS**, crumbled

Serve with warm **FLOUR TORTILLAS** and **PICANTE SAUCE**. Makes a wonderful breakfast or supper. VARIATION: Add $^1/_2$ pound cooked **SAUSAGE.**

EGGS BENEDICTO

Who says English muffins have to be English?

Split and toast	**2 ENGLISH MUFFINS**
Cook until crisp	6 slices **BACON**, cut in half
Poach or fry	4 **EGGS**
Heat together	$^1/_2$ pound **AMERICAN CHEESE**, cubed
	$^1/_4$ cup **PICANTE SAUCE**

Heat until melted. (Use microwave or saucepan.) Presentation: Top each muffin half with 3 slices bacon and 1 egg. Spoon cheese sauce over top. Serve with additional **PICANTE SAUCE**.

HOT TIP

FOR THE MUCHACHOS: Flatten canned BISCUITS into disks. Spread with MARGARINE. Sprinkle with CINNAMON-SUGAR mixture. Bake in preheated 350-degree oven for 5 to 7 minutes until golden brown.

"MAÑANA" CASSEROLE
Make today. Cook and serve "tomorrow".

Grease 13x9x2-inch baking dish. Lightly spread 6 **ENGLISH MUFFIN HALVES** with **MARGARINE**. Place buttered side down in baking dish.

Cook until brown......................	1 pound **PORK SAUSAGE**, crumbled
Drain well.	
Layer $^1/_2$ sausage with $^1/_2$ of	3 cups **CHEDDAR CHEESE**, grated
	1 can (4 oz.) **CHOPPED GREEN CHILIES**
Combine and pour over	12 **EGGS**, beaten
	$1^1/_2$ cups **SOUR CREAM**

Repeat layers sausage, cheese, chilies. Cover and refrigerate 8 hours. Remove from refrigerator and let stand 30 minutes. Bake uncovered, in preheated 350-degree oven for 35 to 40 minutes.

SERAPES DE HUEVOS

Eggs in blankets (taco shells) for morning eye-openers!

Melt in skillet..............................	2 Tbsp. **MARGARINE**
Blend and pour in skillet	10 **EGGS**, beaten
	$1/4$ cup **GREEN ONIONS**, chopped with tops
	$1/2$ cup **PICANTE SAUCE**
	$1/2$ tsp. **SEASONED SALT**

Cook, stirring gently, until eggs are set.

Heat in 350-degree oven ....   10 **TACO SHELLS**

Spoon eggs into each shell. Top with chopped **TOMATO, LETTUCE,** and grated **CHEDDAR CHEESE**. Serve immediately with extra **PICANTE SAUCE** and **FRESH FRUIT.**

HOT TIP

SALSA or PICANTE too HOT!!! Add VINEGAR to "tame".

BRUNCH BURRITOS
Start the day Southwest style.

Place in large skillet .... 2 Tbsp. **MARGARINE**
Cook until tender .... 1 **ONION**, chopped
                                         1 **SWEET PEPPER**, chopped

Combine and add to mix .... 8 **EGGS**, beaten
                                     1 cup grated **CHEDDAR** or **MONTEREY JACK CHEESE**

Cook over low heat, stirring gently, until eggs are set.

Heat in small skillet until warm, 2 cups **PICANTE SAUCE**. Dip 6 (8-inch) **FLOUR TORTILLAS** in picante sauce. Spoon $1/2$ cup egg mixture into center of tortilla. Roll up. Place seam side down in lightly greased baking dish. Top with remaining sauce. Cover with foil. Bake in preheated 350-degree oven for 10 minutes or until hot. May wish to serve with **SOUR CREAM**.

HACIENDA HUEVOS

A.M. or P.M. It's good and easy. Just serve in skillet.

Lightly brown .... ¹/₂ pound **SAUSAGE**, crumbled
Drain well. Add .... 2¹/₂ cups **POTATOES**, peeled and diced
                         1 medium **ONION**, chopped
                         ¹/₂ cup **SALSA** or **PICANTE SAUCE**

Cover and cook about 15 to 20 minutes until potatoes are tender.
Add .... 1 **SWEET PEPPER**, (red if available)

Make 4 indentions in potato mixture with back of spoon. Break 1 **EGG** into each. Cover and cook 3 to 5 minutes until eggs are cooked to desired doneness. Serve with **GUACAMOLE, SALSA,** and **SOUR CREAM**.

PEPPERS vary in degree of "hotness". Add a little at a time.

CHORIZO CON PAPAS

Popular potato and sausage dish.

Remove casing from .... ½ pound **CHORIZO MEXICAN SAUSAGE**
(may use **PORK SAUSAGE**)

Brown in skillet, crumbling with fork as it cooks. Remove from pan and DRAIN.

Heat in skillet .... 6 Tbsp. **CORN OIL**
Add and cook until tender .... 1 large **POTATO**, diced
1 medium **ONION**, diced
1 **SWEET PEPPER**, diced
FRESH JALAPENO, diced
2 **TOMATOES**, chopped
Add sausage and .... 6 **EGGS**, well beaten

Cook until eggs are set. Serve on warm **FLOUR TORTILLAS**. Add **PICANTE SAUCE**. VARIATION: Add ½ cup chopped **PIMIENTOS** and ½ cup grated **CHEDDAR** or **MONTEREY JACK CHEESE**.

MEXICAN COUNTRY BREAKFAST

You will need a two-skillet, two-fisted cook!!

SKILLET #1:
Combine in skillet ....
- 4 cups pre-baked **POTATOES**, cubed
- 2 cans (4 oz. ea.) **CHOPPED GREEN CHILIES**
- 2 **FRESH TOMATOES**, diced
- 1 can (15 oz.) **WHOLE KERNEL CORN**, drained
  CHOPPED TOPS of 10 **FRESH ONIONS**

SKILLET #2:
Fry $^1/_2$ pound **BACON** until crisp. Remove to paper towels. Add $^1/_2$ cup **WATER** to bacon fat to "fry steam" 6 **EGGS**. (Cover skillet with lid.) When eggs are set, remove to platter. Drain skillet and line with 6 **CORN TORTILLAS** that have been sprayed on both sides with cooking spray. Heat. Cover with mixture from skillet #1, sprinkle with crumbled bacon, top with eggs and **GRATED CHEESE**. Heat in preheated 350-degree oven until cheese melts. Cut into pie wedges.

BRUNCH TOSTADAS

A late Sunday morning Southwest treat.

Broil 4 **FLOUR TORTILLAS** until crisp and brown, turning once.

Fry crisp and crumble .... 4 slices **BACON**

Combine and mix well .... 6 **EGGS**, beaten

$^1/_4$ cup **PICANTE SAUCE**

$^1/_2$ cup **GREEN ONIONS**, with tops

SALT

Melt 2 to 3 tablespoons **MARGARINE** in skillet. Add egg mixture. Cook, stirring gently until eggs are set. Spoon mixture onto tortillas to within $^1/_2$-inch of edges. Top with crumbled **BACON,** thin wedges of **TOMATO**, shredded **MONTEREY JACK** or **CHEDDAR CHEESE**. Broil until cheese melts.

FIESTA PIE

Easy quiche-like dish for brunch or supper.

Toss together .... 1 cup **MONTEREY JACK CHEESE**, grated
2 Tbsp. **FLOUR**

Add .... 3 **EGGS**, beaten
1 cup **SALSA** or **PICANTE SAUCE**
$1/2$ cup **SWEET PEPPER**, chopped
$1/2$ cup **HALF** and **HALF CREAM**
4 slices **BACON**, cooked and crumbled
SALT and **PEPPER** to taste

Pour into prepared **PIE CRUST**. Bake in preheated 350-degree oven for 35 to 40 minutes or until set. Remove from oven. Let stand for 10 minutes. Serve with warm **SALSA** or **PICANTE SAUCE**.

MEXICAN FOOD: More flavorful when served piping hot.

JUAREZ QUICHE
Too tired for kitchen duty?? Try this one.

Bake in a microwave pie plate according to directions	1 **PASTRY SHELL**
Grate and sprinkle in bottom of shell	1 cup **CHEDDAR CHEESE**
	1½ cups **MONTEREY JACK CHEESE**
Heat, but do not boil	1 cup **MILK**
	1 can (4 oz.) **CHOPPED GREEN CHILIES**
	SALT and **CUMIN**
Whisk into hot mixture..............	3 **EGGS**, lightly beaten

Pour mixture over cheese. Microwave at 70% power for 10 to 12 minutes, turning every 3 to 4 minutes. Pie will be soft in center but will set up during standing time. Let stand at least 30 minutes.

MAMA'S AND PAPA'S CHORIZO
It's easy to make, good to eat.

MAMA'S:

Mix well...

2 pounds **GROUND BEEF**
3 minced **GARLIC** cloves
2 Tbsp. **CHILI POWDER**
3 Tbsp. **VINEGAR**
1 tsp. ground **COMINO**

Add to taste.....................................
SALT, PEPPER, OREGANO, and **MENUDO SPICE MIX**

Refrigerate overnight. Make 12 or 14 patties and fry until brown.

PAPA'S:

Combine ....

1 pound bulk **PORK SAUSAGE**
1 1/2 Tbsp. **CHILI POWDER**
1 minced clove **GARLIC**
Dash of ground **COMINO, OREGANO**

Refrigerate overnight. Make into 6 or 8 patties and fry until brown.

Main Dishes

▼ ▼ ▼ ▼ ▼ ▼ ▼ ▼ ▼ ▼ ▼ ▼ ▼ ▼ ▼ ▼

FAJITAS

Ya'll Come! Let's have a Cinco de Mayo party.

The Mexican Fah-Hee-ta (skirt steak) is the most requested taco recipe sweeping the country. It is best grilled over a mesquite fire, but are delicious regardless of the type of fire used as long as they are not overcooked. **SKIRT STEAK** is a cheap, tough, piece of meat, but when marinated is very good. "Americanized" fajitas can be made with **ROUND** or **FLANK STEAK**, **CHICKEN**, or **SHRIMP**. Served with varying condiments. **(GUACAMOLE**, sliced **ONIONS**, fresh **CILANTRO**, sliced **JALAPENOS**, grated **MONTEREY JACK CHEESE** and **SOUR CREAM.)** The true Mexican fajita is served on a **WARM FLOUR** or **CORN TORTILLA** with **FRESH PICO DE GALLO**. **(REFRIED BEANS**, optional.) Everyone has their own **MARI-NADE** recipe. The most simple consists of equal parts **LIME JUICE, OIL** and **GARLIC** to taste. (Enough to cover the meat.) Marinate 8 to 24 hours in refrigerator. ALWAYS SLICE ACROSS THE GRAIN.

FAJITA MARINADE

Place 5 pounds **FAJITA MEAT (SKIRT, SIRLOIN**, or **ROUND STEAK)** in a large heavy zip-lock bag.

Mix well.......................................
- 2 Tbsp. **WORCESTERSHIRE SAUCE**
- ³/₄ cup **DRY RED WINE**
- ³/₄ cup **OIL**
- ³/₄ cup **LIME** or **LEMON JUICE**
- 1 small **ONION**, diced
- 2 tsp. **SALT**
- 2 tsp. **COARSE GROUND PEPPER**
- 2 cloves **GARLIC**, pressed
- **OREGANO** (optional)

Marinade meat. Refrigerate 24 hours. Turn several times. Grill steaks over a very hot fire, 4 to 6 minutes per side. **DO NOT OVERCOOK.** Cut steaks in thin strips across the grain. Warm **FLOUR TORTILLAS** on a hot "comal," (iron skillet) or wrap in foil and place on grill while cooking meat. Serve with **FRESH PICO DE GALLO** and condiments of your choice. VARIATION: Substitute ¹/₂ cup **TEQUILA** for **RED WINE**.

SIESTA ROAST N' BEANS
Sleep while it cooks.

Place in a large pan......................	3-4	pound **ROAST**
Place on top of roast	2	cups **PINTO BEANS**, uncooked
	1	can **GREEN CHILIES**, chopped
	1	can **TOMATOES**
	1	**ONION**, chopped
	1	can **TOMATO SAUCE**

Cover entire contents with **WATER**. Place in 250-degree oven covered with lid. Cook at least 12 hours. (May cook longer). Season with **SALT** and **PEPPER**. Serve with **SALAD, CORNBREAD,** and a **DESSERT** for a complete meal.

HOT TIP

'CROSS THE BORDER'S No. 1 hint. Remove papery skins from WHOLE GARLIC. (1 per person.) Drizzle with OIL. Wrap in foil. Bake 2 hours in preheated 275-degree oven. Cut 1/4 off top. Spread on warm TORTILLAS. (For Italian food — spread on FRENCH BREAD.)

MEX-TEX STEAK
Good "ole Gringo" grub!

Brown in skillet ....   4 tenderized, serving size, **CUBED STEAKS** or **ROUND STEAK**
    2 Tbsp. **MARGARINE**

Place in lightly **GREASED** baking dish.

Top with ....   1 can (4 oz.) **CHOPPED GREEN CHILIES**
    1 jar (8 oz.) **TACO SAUCE**

Cover and bake in preheated 350-degree oven for 40 minutes.

Sprinkle with ....   1/2 cup **MONTEREY JACK CHEESE**, grated

Bake uncovered an additional 5 minutes or until cheese is melted.

LONE STAR CASSEROLE
An easy recipe with great results.

Cook and set aside	1 pound **GROUND BEEF**
Season with	1 tsp. **GARLIC SALT**
In separate skillet cook until transparent	³/₄ cup **ONION**, chopped
In	2 Tbsp. **MARGARINE**
Add. Simmer 10 minutes	1 can (15 oz.) **TOMATO SAUCE**
	1 can (4 oz.) **DICED GREEN CHILIES**
	1 tsp. **SALT** and **CUMIN**
	¹/₄ tsp. **RED PEPPER**
Crush and have ready	1 pkg. (8 oz.) **TORTILLA CHIPS**
Grate...	2 cups (8 oz.) **CHEESE**

Layer in a **BUTTERED** 9-inch baking dish. Start with chips, then beef, cheese and sauce. Bake in a preheated 350-degree oven for 20 minutes. Remove from oven.

Spread with	1 cup **SOUR CREAM**
Sprinkle with	¹/₂ cup grated **CHEDDAR CHEESE**

Bake an additional 5 to 10 minutes. Serve with **BEANS** and a **SALAD.**

SOUR CREAM TACOS

Never a bite left.

Brown in medium skillet	1¹/₂ pound **GROUND BEEF**
	3 medium **ONIONS**, chopped
Stir in	2 Tbsp. **CHILI POWDER**
Drain off excess fat. Add	1 can (16 oz.) **TOMATOES**, chopped
	2 or 3 **JALAPENO PEPPERS**, finely chopped
	1 pound **CHEDDAR CHEESE**, grated
	2 cups **SOUR CREAM**
	SALT and **PEPPER** to taste

Mix well and heat (do not boil).
Stir in ....8 to 10 **CORN TORTILLAS**, torn into pieces

Pour mixture into a large greased casserole dish. Bake in preheated 350-degree oven for 30 minutes. This is a good make ahead recipe. Put into two smaller dishes, cook one and freeze the other.

HOT SALSA POT ROAST

The lively, spicy flavor is an unexpected delight.

SALT, PEPPER, and brown
in a large deep pan .... 1 Tbsp. **OIL**
3 pound **ROAST**

Place on top of meat .... 2 **ONIONS**, thick sliced
Combine and
pour over meat .... 1 can (8 oz.) **TOMATO SAUCE**
1 cup **PICANTE SAUCE**
$1^1/_4$ tsp. ground **CUMIN**
$^1/_2$ tsp. **OREGANO LEAVES**, crushed
2 **GARLIC** cloves, minced
$^1/_2$ cup **WATER**

Cover and place in preheated 350-degree oven for $2^1/_2$ to 3 hours or until tender.

During last 15 minutes add .... 1 **GREEN PEPPER**, chopped

Place on platter and cover with remaining sauce from pan.

CHEATERS CHILI RELLENOS
You don't have to fry these.

Rinse and remove
   seeds from .... 4 cans (4 oz.) **WHOLE GREEN CHILIES**, drained

Grate and mix together .... 1½ cups **MONTEREY JACK CHEESE**
1½ cups **CHEDDAR CHEESE**

Stuff each chili with 3 tablespoons cheese. Arrange in bottom of lightly **GREASED** 13x9x2-inch baking dish. Top with remaining cheese.

Combine and mix well .... 6 **EGGS**, beaten
¾ cup **MILK**
SALT and **PEPPER**

Pour over chilies. Bake in preheated 350-degree oven for 30 minutes or until set.
VARIATION: Brown and season 1 pound **GROUND BEEF** and stuff each chili with meat and cheese mixture.

AZTEC ROLL-UPS
A real favorite of ours.

Cook together until meat is done
and vegetables are tender .....
- 1 pound **GROUND BEEF**
- 1 small **ONION**, chopped
- $1/2$ cup **GREEN PEPPER**, chopped
- 1 clove **GARLIC**, minced
- 1 Tbsp. **CHILI POWDER**
- 1 tsp. **SALT**

Stir in ....
- 1 can (8 oz.) **TOMATO SAUCE**
- $1/2$ cup **MILK**
- 2 cups **RICE,** cooked

Heat thoroughly and fold in ..... 1 cup **CHEDDAR CHEESE**, cubed

Roll in warmed **FLOUR TORTILLAS** and serve with **HOT SAUCE**. May serve
piled on top of **CORN CHIPS**.

GRINGOS SPECIALTY

Men like to prepare this green chile casserole for their Super Bowl Gang!

Brown and drain well ....
1 pound lean **GROUND BEEF**
1 medium **ONION**, diced

Add...
1 can (10 oz.) **CREAM OF CHICKEN SOUP**
1 can (10 oz.) **CREAM OF MUSHROOM SOUP**
1 can (10 oz.) chopped **GREEN CHILIES**
1 can (10 oz.) **GREEN CHILI ENCHILADA SAUCE**
1 can (12 oz.) **EVAPORATED MILK**

Lightly oil a 13x9x2-inch baking dish and add 1 large bag **TOSTADO CHIPS**. Pour mixture over chips. Cover with 1 pound grated **SHARP CHEDDAR CHEESE**. Bake in preheated 350-degree oven until hot.

MEXICAN LASAGNA

A well-seasoned dish-great for company.

Brown in skillet .... 1$^1/_2$ pounds **GROUND MEAT**
1 **ONION**, chopped
Add .... 2 cloves **GARLIC**, minced
2 cans (16 oz.) **TOMATOES**
1$^1/_2$ tsp. **TACO SEASONING**
SALT and **PEPPER**
Have ready .... 8 ounces **COTTAGE CHEESE**
1 cup **CHEDDAR CHEESE**, grated
$^3/_4$ pound **MONTEREY JACK CHEESE**, grated
Tear into pieces .... 8 **CORN TORTILLAS**

Layer in a 13x9x2-inch pan, starting with tortillas, meat, cottage cheese, cheddar cheese and top with monterey jack cheese. Sprinkle with sliced **BLACK OLIVES**. Bake in preheated 350-degree oven for 1 hour.

MAMA MIAS TACO PIZZA

Disappears fast around little muchachos.

Combine ....
2 cups **BISCUIT MIX**
$^1/_2$ cup cold **WATER**

Pat dough evenly into GREASED 12-inch pizza pan. Form $^1/_2$-inch edge; prick bottom and sides with a fork. Bake in preheated 425-degree oven for 10 minutes until crust is browned. Set aside.

In skillet brown and
   stir to crumble ....
1 pound **GROUND BEEF**

Add. Simmer 5 minutes ....
1 cup **WATER**
1 pkg. (1$^1/_4$ ozs.) **TACO SEASONING MIX**
1 can (15$^1/_2$ oz.) **MEXICAN-STYLE CHILI BEANS**

Spoon over crust. Top with ......
1 cup **CHEDDAR CHEESE**, grated

Bake 5 more minutes. Remove. Top with 1 cup crushed **TORTILLA CHIPS**, shredded **LETTUCE,** chopped **TOMATOES** and chopped **GREEN ONIONS.**

Slice and serve immediately with **TACO SAUCE.**

▼ ▼ ▼ ▼ ▼ ▼ ▼ ▼ ▼ ▼ ▼ ▼ ▼ ▼ ▼ ▼ 45

DEEP-DISH MEXICAN MEAT PIE

A satisfying easy-to-prepare meal.

Thaw and bake
   for 10 minutes .... 2 frozen **PIE SHELLS**
Mix together .... 1 can (16 oz.) **REFRIED BEANS**
                              $^1/_2$ cup **PICANTE SAUCE**

Spread $^1/_2$ in bottom of each pie shell.
Brown in skillet .... 1 pound **GROUND MEAT**
With .... 1 small **ONION**, chopped
                              $^1/_2$ tsp. **SALT**
                              1 package ($1^1/_4$ oz.) **TACO SEASONING**

Divide and spread on top of bean mixture.
Top each with $^1/_2$ of .... 1 cup crushed **TORTILLA CHIPS**
                              2 cups **CHEDDAR CHEESE**, grated
Circle edge of pies with .... 1 can (4 oz.) **CHOPPED GREEN CHILIES**

Bake in preheated 350-degree oven 20 - 25 minutes. To serve sprinkle with chopped
TOMATOES and **GREEN ONIONS**. VARIATION: For thicker pie use 1 large **DEEP-DISH PIE SHELL**.

CARNE GUISADA
A shin-kicking, rib sticking helluva dish!

Slightly brown in saucepan	2 pounds **ROUND STEAK**, cubed and floured
	1/4 cup **OIL**
Chop and add the following	1/4 **GREEN PEPPER**
	1/4 **ONION**
	1 **TOMATO**
	1 fresh **JALAPENO**, seeded
	2 cloves **GARLIC**
Add..	1/2 tsp. **GROUND CUMIN**
	1/2 Tbsp. **CHILI POWDER**
	SALT and **PEPPER**
	1 can (14 oz.) **BEEF BROTH**, or **WATER**

Cover, simmer gently 2 hours or until very tender. Add broth or water as needed. Serve over **WHITE RICE**. For a wonderful meal add **PINTO BEANS** and **GUACAMOLE**.

BEEF AND CHEESE ENCHILADAS
Popular recipe from More Calf Fries to Caviar.

Brown in skillet	1 pound **EXTRA LEAN GROUND BEEF**
Drain well and set aside.	
Grate	10 ounces **CHEDDAR CHEESE**
Chop	1 **ONION** (Saute with beef if you prefer your onions cooked.)

Place 2 tablespoons meat in a **CORN TORTILLA.** Sprinkle with cheese and onion. Roll up tight and place in a slightly greased 13x9x2-inch baking dish, seam side down. (To soften tortillas, dip into $1/4$-inch hot grease for just a minute on each side, so that they will be more pliable. Or, wrap loosely in plastic wrap and microwave 30 seconds.) Cover with **SAUCE** (recipe follows).

SAUCE:

Melt in saucepan	$^1/_2$ cup **MARGARINE**
Add..	3 Tbsp. **FLOUR**
Gradually add	2 cups **MILK**
Cook until slightly thickened ...	8 ounces **VELVEETA CHEESE**
Add..	1 can **CHOPPED CHILIES**

Pour over filled tortillas. Cover with grated **AMERICAN CHEESE**. Cover with foil and bake in preheated oven at 350-degrees for 15 minutes. Make ahead of time and freeze for those drop-in guests. VARIATION: Cooked **CHICKEN** or **SHRIMP** may be substituted for ground meat. Also, try just plain **CHEESE** for filling.

Make enchiladas with half FLOUR TORTILLAS and half CORN TORTILLAS. This makes everyone happy.

LAREDO MEAT PIE
This is a robust one-dish meal.

Brown in skillet .... 1 pound **GROUND MEAT**
$^1/_2$ cup chopped **ONION**

Add .... 2 Tbsp. **CHILI POWDER**
$1^1/_2$ tsp. **SALT**
1 Tbsp. **WORCESTERSHIRE SAUCE**
1 cup **TOMATOES**, chopped

Cover and simmer over low heat
for 15 minutes. Add .... 1 cup **PINTO BEANS**, cooked or canned
Pour into greased baking dish.
Top with .... $1^1/_2$ cups **CORNBREAD BATTER**

Carefully spread with a wet knife. Bake in a preheated 425-degree oven for 20 to 30 minutes, or until cornbread is browned.

CHOPPED ONIONS added to a casserole have best flavor if browned first.

ETTA-RITA'S SPANISH NOODLES
This will feed a whole bunch of ya'll.

Brown in skillet	2 pounds lean **GROUND PORK**
	1/4 cup **MARGARINE, SALT** and **PEPPER**
Add	1 **ONION**, chopped
	3 stalks **CELERY**, chopped
	1 **GREEN PEPPER**, chopped
When slightly cooked add	1 can (15 oz.) **TOMATOES**
	1 can (10 oz.) **TOMATOES AND GREEN CHILIES**
Season to taste with	**CHILI POWDER**
Simmer for 1 hour.	
Have ready	1 pound **CHEDDAR CHEESE**, grated
Cook according to package until slightly soft. Then drain	2 pkgs. (8 oz.) **EGG NOODLES**

Mix all together. Pour into large greased baking dish or two smaller ones. Bake in preheated 350-degree oven until cheese is melted. Freezes well.

▼ ▼ ▼ ▼ ▼ ▼ ▼ ▼ ▼ ▼ ▼ ▼ ▼ ▼ ▼ ▼ ▼ ▼ 51

MEXICAN PORK CHOPS AND BEANS

Not even a pot to wash.

Place a large **OVEN COOKING BAG** in a 13x9x2-inch baking pan.

Add to bag and shake	2 Tbsp. **FLOUR**
Then add	1 cup **SALSA**
	2 Tbsp. **LIME JUICE**
	1 tsp. **CHILI POWDER**
	1 1/2 tsp. **GARLIC SALT**
	1/2 tsp. **CUMIN**

Squeeze bag to mix.

Place in bag	4 1/2-inch thick, fat trimmed **PORK CHOPS**
Spoon around chops	1 **ONION**, chopped
	2 **GREEN PEPPERS**, cubed
	1 can (16 oz.) **PINTO BEANS**, drained

Close bag with nylon tie. Cut 6 half-inch slits in top. Bake in preheated 350-degree oven for about 35 minutes. Let stand in bag 5 minutes before serving.

PANCHOS CHALUPES
Makes a great simple party.

Place in a large pot .... 3 pound boneless **PORK ROAST**
1 pound **DRIED PINTO BEANS**
7 cups **WATER**
2 **ONIONS**, chopped
2 cloves **GARLIC**, chopped
3 Tbsp. **CHILI POWDER**
1 Tbsp. **GROUND CUMIN**
1 tsp. **OREGANO**
1 can (4 oz.) **CHOPPED GREEN CHILIES**

Cover, cook over low heat for 5 hours. (May cook in a 250-degree oven.) When cooked shred meat with a fork. Spoon over crisp fried **CORN** or **FLOUR TORTIL-LAS**. Let everyone choose their own condiments. Have bowls of toppings to choose from. Our favorites: shredded **LETTUCE**, chopped **ONIONS**, chopped **TOMATOES**, **GUACAMOLE**, **SOUR CREAM,** grated **CHEESE** and **PICANTE SAUCE**.

CHEESY 'CHILADA CASSEROLE

A complete meal. Ideal for busy cooks.

Have ready .... 12 **CORN TORTILLAS**
2 cups **CHEDDAR CHEESE**, grated
Brown in 10-inch skillet .... 1 pound ground **PORK** or **BEEF**
1 **ONION**, chopped
1 **GREEN PEPPER**, chopped
1 clove **GARLIC**, minced
Add .... 1 can (15 oz.) **PINTO BEANS**, drained
1 can (15 oz.) **TOMATO SAUCE**
1 cup **PICANTE SAUCE**
1 tsp. ground **CUMIN** (optional)

Simmer 15 minutes. Cover bottom of a 9x13x2-inch baking dish with 6 tortillas. Top with one-half meat mixture; sprinkle with 1 cup cheese. Layer remaining ingredients. Cover tightly with aluminum foil; bake in preheated 350-degree oven for 25 minutes. To serve, top with **LETTUCE**, **TOMATO**, and **SOUR CREAM**.

NORTH OF THE BORDER STUFFED QUAIL
Makes the hunting an extra special treat.

Separate and remove bone from breasts of 2 dozen (fresh or frozen) **QUAIL**. Make a slit in each and insert a $1^1/_2$x$^1/_2$-inch piece of **MONTEREY JACK CHEESE** and $^1/_2$ of a **JALAPENO PEPPER**. (Fresh or canned, halved and seeded.) Wrap slice of **PEPPERED BACON** around breasts to enclose. Secure with a toothpick. Cook on hot grill, turning to brown. Quail will cook in approximately 30 minutes. VARIATION: Substitute **BONELESS CHICKEN THIGHS** for the Quail. Chicken will need to cook longer. Approximately 40 to 45 minutes.

 HOT TIP

BEST SEASONING IN SOUTHWEST: Mix well, equal parts of PAPRIKA, CAYENNE, LEMON PEPPER, GARLIC POWDER, CUMIN and CHILI POWDER. Store in tight container. Great seasoning for Mexican foods.

SHRIMP OLÉ
A quick and easy recipe for a busy schedule.

Prepare **MINUTE** or **REGULAR RICE** for four to six people, according to directions. Set aside.

Peel and devein **SHRIMP**. Cover with water and steam approximately 15 minutes for medium size shrimp. (Cook about 6 to 8 shrimp per person.) Set aside.

Mix together and
    heat until melted ....   1 can (10 oz.) **TOMATOES** and **CHOPPED CHILIES**
                                       1 pound **VELVEETA CHEESE**

Presentation: Place 1 serving of rice in center of plate. Place boiled shrimp over rice. Cover with the cheese mixture. Surround with **GREEN SALAD.** Serve with **HOT BREAD**.

TEJAS PEPPERED SHRIMP
One of the great discoveries.

Mix together in large skillet,
  cover and steam
  15 to 30 minutes .... 36 to 40 **SHRIMP** (remove heads but leave in shells)
                    $^1/_2$ cup **MARGARINE**
                     1 **LEMON**, sliced very thin (leave rind on)
     $^1/_2$ to $^3/_4$ cup **WHITE WINE**
                      SALT
                      LOTS OF CRACKED PEPPER

Serve warm in shells with **SALSA** or **COCKTAIL SAUCE**.

 HOT TIP

SUMMER SALAD . . . Halve, seed and peel a RIPE AVOCADO. Fill with PICANTE or SALSA. Top with cooked CRAB MEAT or SHRIMP. Serve on LETTUCE LEAF.

▼ ▼ ▼ ▼ ▼ ▼ ▼ ▼ ▼ ▼ ▼ ▼ ▼ ▼ ▼ ▼   57

SHRIMP DE SENORA WORLEY
Seafood recipe from the Arizona desert?? And it is super good!

Buy **LARGE SHRIMP**. Remove shell, but leave tails attached. Butterfly. (Split down vein almost completely through the shrimp. Remove vein.) Place strip of **FRESH JALAPENO**, strip of **MONTEREY JACK CHEESE** in slit in **SHRIMP**. Close and wrap with approximately $1/2$ strip of **BACON.** Skewer and place on outside grill. Cook 3 to 4 minutes on each side, or until bacon is crisp. (May cook under broiler in conventional oven. Watch carefully so that bacon does not burn.)

ALWAYS seed and remove membranes from JALAPENOS. Less hot and more flavorful.

TEX-MEX HASH

An easy recipe with great results.

Heat in large skillet	1 Tbsp. **OIL**
Add and cook until tender	1 **GREEN PEPPER**, chopped
	2 cups **ONION**, chopped
	1 pound lean **GROUND BEEF**
	1 can (15 oz.**)** **TOMATOES**
	$^1/_2$ cup uncooked **RICE**
	1 tsp. **CHILI POWDER**
	1 tsp. **SALT**
	1 tsp. **GARLIC POWDER**

Mix well, pour into baking dish and cover. Bake in preheated 350-degree oven for 45 minutes or until rice is cooked. Top with grated **CHEDDAR CHEESE**. Return to oven until cheese is melted.

QUICK CHICKEN CASSEROLE
The taste of chicken enchiladas without the trouble.

OIL oven-proof 9x13x2-inch dish. Line with **TOSTADO CHIPS.**

Make a mixture of......................
2 **CHICKENS**, cooked and deboned
(May use canned chicken)
2 cans (10 oz. **CREAM OF MUSHROOM SOUP**
1 cup **HALF** and **HALF CREAM**
1 can (10 oz.) **MILD ENCHILADA SAUCE**
1 cup **MUSHROOMS**
1 tsp. **CHILI POWDER**
$^1/_2$ tsp. **GARLIC SALT**

Pour $^1/_2$ over tostado chips. Repeat.

Top with ....
8 ounces **CHEDDAR CHEESE**, grated

Bake in preheated 350-degree oven until thoroughly heated.

HOT TIP

Bake and serve in individual Mexican casserole dishes.

NORTH-OF-THE-BORDER CHICKEN CASSEROLE
Good family dish. Make Two. Freeze One.

Boil, debone and chop...............	1 **CHICKEN**
Mix in bowl...............................	1 cup **CHICKEN BROTH**
	1 can (10 oz.) **CREAM OF MUSHROOM SOUP**
	1 can (10 oz.) **CREAM OF CHICKEN SOUP**
	1 can (4 oz.) **CHOPPED GREEN CHILIES**
	1 tsp. **CHILI POWDER**
	1 **ONION**, chopped
	1/4 tsp. each, **GARLIC SALT, PEPPER** and **TABASCO SAUCE**
Have ready..................................	4 cups **CORN CHIPS**
Grate..	8 oz. **CHEDDAR CHEESE**

Lightly **GREASE** bottom of a 3-quart casserole dish. Spread half of each in order given, chips, chicken, sauce and cheese. Repeat. Ending with cheese. Bake in preheated 350-degree oven for 30 minutes or until hot.

▼ ▼ ▼ ▼ ▼ ▼ ▼ ▼ ▼ ▼ ▼ ▼ ▼ ▼ ▼ ▼ ▼ ▼

SAN ANTONIO SOFT CHICKEN TACOS
A Riverwalk Specialty!

Cook 1 **CHICKEN** in water seasoned with **GARLIC** and **SEASONED SALT**. Remove bone and shred.

Heat in skillet .... 1 Tbsp. **OIL**

Add .... 1 can (13 oz.) **TOMATOES**, chopped
1 tsp. **GARLIC POWDER**
2 tsp. **CUMIN**
SALT and **PEPPER**

Add chicken. Use as filling for warmed **CORN** or **FLOUR TORTILLAS.** Make extra and freeze.

Use for CHICKEN NACHOS or CRISPY TACOS. (If chicken is large, add more seasoning.)

CHICKEN VERRRRY HOT!!!!
Verrrry true!!!

Cook, debone, and chop ....   1 large **CHICKEN**

Arrange in a 9x13x2-inch baking dish.

Layer ....   1 large **ONION**, chopped
$1^1/_2$ cups **CHEDDAR CHEESE**, grated
$^1/_3$ cup **CHOPPED RIPE OLIVES**
2 cups **TORTILLA CHIPS**, broken up

Combine ....   1 can (10 oz.) **CREAM CHICKEN SOUP**
1 can (10 oz.) **CREAM MUSHROOM SOUP**
1 can (10 oz.) **TOMATOES** and **CHILIES**

Pour over layered mixture. Bake in preheated 325-degree oven for 30 to 40 minutes until bubbly. Garnish with **RIPE OLIVES.**

CHICKEN ENCHILADAS
Perfect fare for a Mexican Fiesta.

Boil, debone and cube	5 whole **CHICKEN BREASTS**
Add and heat together	2 cans (10 oz.) **CREAM OF CHICKEN SOUP**
	2 cups **SOUR CREAM**
	1 bunch **GREEN ONIONS**, chopped
	1 can (8 oz.) **DICED GREEN CHILIES**
	1/4 tsp. **CHILI POWDER**
	SALT and **PEPPER** to taste
Heat to soften	12 **CORN TORTILLAS**
Have grated and ready	3 cups **MONTEREY JACK CHEESE**

Place 1 tablespoon chicken mixture in tortilla. Sprinkle with cheese. Roll and place seam side down in dish. If any chicken is left pour it over the enchiladas. Top with more cheese. Bake in preheated 350-degree oven 45 minutes.

SENOR LOPEZ' MAIN DISH
Good choice!   (He's dieting.)

Heat in a 10-inch skillet	2 tsp. **MARGARINE**
Add and cook 10 minutes turning once	2 whole **CHICKEN** breast, split, deboned and skinned
Seasoned with	**GARLIC SALT** and **PEPPER**
Spread around edge of skillet ...	$^1/_2$ cup chopped **GREEN ONIONS**
	$^1/_2$ cup chopped **GREEN PEPPER**

Cook 10 minutes or until chicken is done.

Have ready	2 cups hot cooked **RICE**

Place on serving platter. Add chicken. Keep warm.

Leave remainder in skillet, add	$^3/_4$ cup **PICANTE SAUCE**
	4 ounces light **VELVEETA CHEESE**

Cook and stir until cheese is melted and hot. Pour over chicken and rice.

SOUTHWEST SKILLET CHICKEN
So Quick. SOOO Good!!

Debone and skin	4 **CHICKEN BREASTS**
Sprinkle generously with	**GROUND CUMIN** and **SALT**
Brown about 4 minutes per side	
in a medium skillet with........	2 Tbsp. **MARGARINE**
Pour over chicken	1 cup **PICANTE SAUCE**

Cover and simmer 8 to 10 minutes or until tender. Place chicken on serving plate.

Whisk into remaining sauce ..... 4 Tbsp. **SOUR CREAM**

Spoon over chicken. Top with sliced **AVOCADO**. Adjust amounts to number of people.

HOT TIP

HURRY-UP FILLING: Simmer 5 minutes, 3 cups shredded cooked CHICKEN, 4 chopped GREEN ONIONS, 3/4 cup PICANTE SAUCE, 1/2 tsp. CUMIN and OREGANO. Serve as filling for TACOS, TOSDADAS or BURRITOS.

CHICKEN SANTA FE
Make it once, you will make it often!

Cut into 1-inch strips..................	3 **CHICKEN BREASTS**
Seasoned with..............................	**SALT, PEPPER** and **GARLIC SALT**
Slightly brown in	1/4 cup **OIL**
Add and cook until soft	1 cup **ONION**, chopped
	1/2 cup **BELL PEPPER**, chopped
Then, add	1 can (10 oz.) **TOMATOES** and **GREEN CHILIES**
	1 cup **WATER**
	1 tsp. **GARLIC SALT**
	1/2 tsp. **PEPPER**
	1/4 tsp. **CUMIN**
	1 1/2 cup **MINUTE RICE**

Bring to boil. Cover. Set aside until rice is done. Place in greased casserole dish. Cover with grated **MOZZARELLA CHEESE**. Heat in preheated 350-degree oven long enough to melt cheese. Serve with **BREAD** and **SALAD**.

CHICKEN FAJITAS
As Tex-Mex as the Rio Grande.

Skin .... 2 to 3 pounds boneless **CHICKEN BREASTS**

Rub well with dry **FAJITA SEASONING** and place in heavy zip-lock bag.

Combine .... 1 bottle (8 oz.) **ZESTY ITALIAN DRESSING**
$^1/_2$ cup **WHITE WINE**

Pour over chicken breasts. Marinate in refrigerator 12 to 14 hours. Heat grill. Cook chicken over hot coals for 5 to 8 minutes per side, depending on thickness of meat. Baste with marinade. **DO NOT OVERCOOK.** Slice into lengthwise strips. Warm **FLOUR TORTILLAS**. Place chicken in middle of **TORTILLA** and scatter sauteed **ONION SLICES** on top. Fold over and serve with **FRESH PICO DE GALLO** and condiments of your choice.

WARM TORTILLAS . . . wrap loosely in plastic wrap, microwave 1 minute. Or wrap in foil and heat in 350-degree oven 15 minutes.

Soups/Sandwiches

TAOS TACOS

Tacos are the best known and loved "sandwiches".

Brown in skillet .... 1 lb. lean **GROUND BEEF**
With .... 1 **ONION**, chopped
$^1/_2$ tsp. each **SALT, PEPPER, GARLIC SALT, CUMIN**

Cook until meat is done. Drain.
Warm in oven .... 8 ready made **TACO SHELLS**

Or fry your own with **CORN TORTILLAS.**
Fill each prepared shell with meat.
Have ready .... 2 cups **LETTUCE**, shredded
2 **TOMATOES**, chopped
2 cups **CHEESE**, grated

Just before serving add lettuce, tomatoes and cheese. Serve with **SALSA**. For a complete meal, serve with a side dish of **REFRIED BEANS** or **MEXICAN RICE**.

DEL RIO CHIMICHANGAS

A burrito that has been deep fried.

Cook until brown ....   2 cups diced **PORK, CHICKEN,** or **BEEF**

         $^1/_4$ cup **ONION**, chopped

Stir in ....   1 cup **PICANTE SAUCE**

         1 cup **TOMATO SAUCE**

         $^1/_4$ cup **RAISINS** (opt.)

         2 tsp. **CHILI POWDER**

         $^1/_4$ tsp. **CINNAMON**

Cook, stirring often, until very little liquid remains. Let cool. Heat to soften 10 to 12 **TORTILLAS**. Spoon 3 to 4 tablespoons of meat mixture on lower half of each tortilla. Fold two opposite sides toward center. Roll up from bottom. Pour **OIL** into deep heavy skillet to about $^1/_2$-inch in depth. Heat to 350-degrees. Add rolled chimichangas, seam side down. Fry until golden brown, turning once. Drain on paper towels. Top with shredded **LETTUCE**, **SOUR CREAM** sliced **AVOCADO** or **GUACAMOLE.**

MONTEREY BUNWICHES
*For a little extra kick, add diced **JALAPENOS.***

Brown in .... 1 Tbsp. **OIL**
1 pound **GROUND BEEF**
1 cup **ONION**, chopped
1 cup **CELERY**, chopped
Stir to separate meat, add .... 1 tsp. **CHILI POWDER**
$^1/_2$ tsp. **SALT** and **PEPPER**
2 tsp. **HOT CHILI SAUCE**
Add and simmer 15 minutes .... 1 can ($10^1/_2$ oz.) **TOMATO SAUCE**

Serve on toasted **HAMBURGER BUNS.**

MEXI-BURGERS

Turn your hamburger cook-out into a Mexican fiesta!

Mix together .... 1^1/$_2$ pounds **GROUND BEEF**
4 Tbsp. chopped **ONION**
3 Tbsp. diced **GREEN CHILIES**
^{1}/$_2$ tsp. each **SALT, GARLIC SALT, PEPPER**
^{1}/$_4$ tsp. each **CUMIN** and **PAPRIKA**

Form into 6 patties. Cook on grill or fry over medium heat. Serve on warm **HAMBURGER BUNS** with sliced **AVOCADO**.

TORTILLA BURGERS: Substitute warm large FLOUR TORTILLAS for hamburger buns. Fold over cooked HAMBURGER patties. Sprinkle with grated CHEESE, chopped LETTUCE and TOMATOES, and PICANTE SAUCE.

BEEF BURRITOS
Rolled sandwiches.

Warm	2 cups cooked **BEEF**, shredded
	1 cup **REFRIED BEANS**
Warm	8 (10-inch) **FLOUR TORTILLAS**
Have prepared	1 cup **CHEDDAR CHEESE**, grated
	2 cups shredded **LETTUCE**
	2 **TOMATOES**, chopped

Spread 2 tablespoons beans on each tortilla, cover with $1/4$ cup beef. Top with cheese, lettuce and tomatoes. Fold one end of tortilla over filling: roll. To heat omit lettuce and tomatoes, wrap in foil and heat in preheated 350-degree oven for 15 minutes or wrap loosely in plastic wrap and cook in microwave for 30 seconds. VARIATION: Try **BEANS** and **CHEESE.** Cooked **CHICKEN. GROUND BEEF** with **TACO SEASONING.** Or **EGGS** with **SAUSAGE** or **BACON.**

TOSTADAS

A wonderful open faced Mexican sandwich!

Fry until crisp .... **TORTILLAS**
Cover with warmed .... **REFRIED BEANS**
Sprinkle on generous
   amounts of .... **CHEDDAR** or **JACK CHEESE**, grated
Chop and cover with .... **LETTUCE, TOMATOES** and **AVOCADOS**

A nice blob of **SOUR CREAM** and a spoon of **PICANTE SAUCE** tops off this wonderful creation. Messy. Have plenty of napkins handy. (Good with meat, also.)

MINI-TOSTADAS. Place REFRIED BEANS on TORTILLA CHIPS. Heat in oven. Garnish with grated CHEESE, GUACAMOLE, SALSA, etc.

▼ ▼ ▼ ▼ ▼ ▼ ▼ ▼ ▼ ▼ ▼ ▼ ▼ ▼ ▼ ▼   75

QUICK-TO-FIX-QUESADILLAS
No-fuss cooking!

Have ready .... 3 10-inch **FLOUR TORTILLAS**
2 cups **CHEDDAR CHEESE**, grated
1 can (4 oz.) **DICED GREEN CHILIES**

In heavy skillet start layering in order given, starting with one tortilla. Use one third of cheese and chilies. Continue stacking until you have three layers. Cover and cook until cheese is melted. Cut into 6 wedges. Serve with a dollop of **SOUR CREAM** and **SALSA** on each wedge. For an outdoor party stack on heavy duty foil, seal and place on grill to heat. VARIATION: Add shredded cooked **CHICKEN** or **HAMBURGER MEAT**.

DOS AMIGOS TACO SOUP
Two of our best friends submitted this recipe.

Brown together in large pot	2 lbs. lean **GROUND BEEF**
	1 **ONION**, chopped
	SALT and **PEPPER**
Add and cook 1 minute	1 Tbsp. **CHILI POWDER**
	1 pkg. dry **TACO MIX**
Add..	2 cans (16 oz. ea.) **TOMATOES**, chopped
	2 cans (15 oz. ea.) **RANCH STYLE BEANS**
	1 can (15 oz.) **JALAPENO PINTO BEANS**
	1 can (15 oz.) **HOMINY**
	1 can (15 oz.) whole kernel **CORN**
	1 can (4 oz.) **CHOPPED GREEN CHILIES**
Optional..	1 pkg. **RANCH DRESSING**, dry

Simmer for about 30 minutes. Serve in bowls with a topping of grated **CHEDDAR CHEESE**, a spot of **SOUR CREAM** and a sprinkle of fresh **CHIVES.**

MEXICAN CHOWDER
Colorful, Tasty. A winner everytime.

In a skillet brown	1/2 pound **BULK PORK SAUSAGE**
Drain well. Pour into a large pot and add	2 cups **PINTO BEANS**, cooked or canned
	1 1/2 cups chopped **TOMATOES**
	2 cups **WATER**
	1 **ONION**, chopped
	1 **BAY LEAF**
	1/2 tsp. **SALT, GARLIC SALT**
	1/4 tsp. **THYME, PEPPER**
Simmer for 1 hour. Add	1/2 cup diced **POTATOES**
	1/4 cup chopped **GREEN PEPPER**

Cook 15 minutes more. Remove bay leaf and serve.

CREAMY AZTEC SOUP

Simmering soups are ideal winter warmers.

Brown together in large pot	1¹/₂ pound **GROUND BEEF**
	1 **ONION**, chopped
Drain and add	1 can (15 oz.) **CHILI**, no beans
	1 can (15 oz.) **STEWED TOMATOES**
	2 cans (16 oz. ea.) **PINTO BEANS**
	1 can (10 oz.) **TOMATOES** and **GREEN CHILIES**
Mix well and stir in	1 pound **VELVEETA**, diced
	1 pint **SOUR CREAM**

Simmer for 30 minutes. Stir occasionally. Serve in bowls over **CORN CHIPS.**

RIO GRANDE CHILI

Hot, spicy and delicious on a cold winter day!

Brown in large pot .... 4 pounds lean **GROUND CHILI MEAT**
1 **ONION**, chopped

Drain. Add .... 3 cloves **GARLIC**, minced
5 Tbsp. **CHILI POWDER**
4 tsp. **CUMIN**
5 Tbsp. **PAPRIKA**
SALT and **PEPPER**
2 cans (7 1/2 oz. ea.) **TOMATO SAUCE**
2 cans (13 oz. ea.) **TOMATO JUICE**

Use sparingly to taste .... **GROUND RED PEPPER**

Add small amounts of **WATER** at a time to keep at desired thickness and to prevent sticking. Simmer for 1 hour, stirring often.

TORTILLA SOUP

If you've never had tortilla soup, you're in for a real treat.

Heat in large pan	2 Tbsp. **OIL**
Add and cook until soft	1 **ONION**, chopped
Add	2 cloves **GARLIC**, minced
	1 can (4 oz.) **CHOPPED GREEN CHILIES**
	2 cans (15 oz. ea.) **STEWED TOMATOES**
	1 can (11 oz.) **TOMATO SOUP**
	1 can (15 oz.) **BEEF BROTH**
	1 can (15 oz.) **CHICKEN BROTH**
	2 tsp. **WORCESTERSHIRE SAUCE**
	1 tsp. each **SALT, CHILI POWDER, CUMIN, SUGAR, PEPPER**
	$1^1/_4$ tsp. **TABASCO SAUCE**
	$1^1/_2$ cups **WATER**
	1 cup **CHICKEN**, cooked, chopped

Simmer for one hour. To serve spoon over **TORTILLA CHIPS** in bottom of each bowl. Cover with hot soup, grated **CHEDDAR CHEESE** and chopped **AVOCADO**.

▼ ▼ ▼ ▼ ▼ ▼ ▼ ▼ ▼ ▼ ▼ ▼ ▼ ▼ ▼ ▼ ▼

ENCHILADA SOUP

A Low Cal wonderful creamy soup. Freezes well.

Cook in 16 cups **WATER**........... 3 pounds **CHICKEN BREAST**
Save all of the broth for later. Chop chicken and set aside.
Melt in separate pan................. 1 cup **MARGARINE**
Add and cook until tender........ 1 **ONION**, chopped
2 cloves **GARLIC**, minced
3 stalks **CELERY**, diced
Gradually add .... 1¹/₂ cups **FLOUR**
2 tsp. **PAPRIKA**
2 tsp. **SEASONING SALT**
Slowly add reserved broth. Cook until thickened, stirring constantly.
Add................................ ¹/₄ tsp. **CUMIN**
1 can (15 oz.) **TOMATOES**, chopped
1 can (8 oz.) diced **CARROTS**
1 can (8 oz.) **CHOPPED GREEN CHILIES**
2 pints **SOUR CREAM**
Add chicken. Serve over crunched **TORTILLA CHIPS** in individual bowls. Sprinkle
with grated **CHEESE** and chopped **FRESH GREEN ONIONS**. Large recipe.

RANCHO RIO TACO SOUP

Easy as 1-2-3.

Cook until brown........................   1 1/2 pounds lean **GROUND BEEF**
                                              1/4 cup **ONION**, chopped
Add and simmer 30 minutes ....   1 can (16 oz.) **STEWED TOMATOES**
                                               1 can (8 oz.) **TOMATO SAUCE**
                                               1 package **TACO SEASONING**

Pour over small **CORN CHIPS** in bowls. Add a layer of grated **CHEDDAR CHEESE**.
Garnish with chopped **FRESH ONIONS** and chopped **AVOCADO.**

TEXAS TOUCH! Cook favorite CHILI. Add PICANTE SAUCE to taste.
Pour over CRUSHED CORN CHIPS Top with grated CHEESE.

EASY TORTILLA SOUP
This is a tasty light soup.

Blend until chunky	1 can (14¹/₂ oz.) **TOMATOES**
	1 **ONION**, diced
	1 clove **GARLIC**, minced
	2 Tbsp. **CILANTRO** or **PARSLEY**
	¹/₄ tsp. **SUGAR**
Pour into saucepan. Add	5 cups **CHICKEN BROTH**
	SALT and **PEPPER**
Simmer 20 minutes.	
Have ready	2 cups **MONTEREY JACK CHEESE,** cubed
	2 **AVOCADOS**, cubed
	8 ounces **FRIED CORN TORTILLA CHIPS**, broken

To serve, place cubed cheese, avocado and tortilla chips in bottom of each bowl. Pour very hot soup in bowls.

SANTA FE POSOLE

A New Year's Day tradition in Mexico.

In a large pot cook until done...	3 pounds **PORK**, cut into chunks
In	6 cups **WATER**
Seasoned with...........................	1^1/$_2$ tsp. **SALT**
When tender add	1 **ONION**, chopped
	6 cups **POSOLE** or 3 cans (15 oz. ea.) **HOMINY**
	1 can (15 oz.) **PINTO BEANS**
	2 cloves **GARLIC**, minced
	1 tsp. **OREGANO**
	2 Tbsp. **CHILI POWDER**
	^{1}/$_2$ tsp. each **SALT, PEPPER** and **GARLIC SALT**

Simmer one hour before serving. (Remove bones!) If using frozen posole cook in pot with pork. Posole pops into hominy when done. Serve with **MEXICAN CORNBREAD**.

GAZPACHO

A cool refreshing soup. Great for summertime.

Chop together .... 1 medium **ONION**
1 **GREEN BELL PEPPER**
1 **CUCUMBER**, peeled
3 **TOMATOES**, peeled

Place in large container. Add ... 1 can (46 oz.) **TOMATO JUICE**
$1/4$ cup **RED WINE VINEGAR**
2 Tbsp. **LEMON JUICE**
$1/4$ cup **OLIVE OIL**
2 Tbsp. **WORCESTERSHIRE SAUCE**
$1/2$ tsp. **SALT**
$1/8$ tsp. **CAYENNE PEPPER**
BLACK PEPPER

Mix well. Cover and chill before serving. Will keep up to two weeks refrigerated.

GRINGO BEAN SOUP
Twenty minutes from start to finish

Chop and fry until crisp .... 4 slices **BACON**
Add .... 1 **ONION**, chopped
1 **GREEN PEPPER**, chopped
3 cloves **GARLIC**, minced

Cover and cook over low heat for 15 minutes.
Add .... 1 can (14 oz.) **CHICKEN BROTH**
1 can (16 oz.) **REFRIED BEANS**
1 can (4 oz.) **CHOPPED GREEN CHILIES**
1 Tbsp. **CHILI POWDER**
1 tsp. **SALT**
1 Tbsp. **SALSA**, or to taste

Bring to a boil, simmer 10 minutes. Serve in individual bowls, topped with **GRATED CHEESE.**

BLACK BEAN SOUP
A favorite in the Southwest.

Cover with **WATER.**

Soak overnight	2 cups **BLACK BEANS**
Drain. Cover with	5 cups **WATER**
Add and simmer 2 hours...........	1/4 pound **HAM** or **SALT PORK**
Add..	1 **ONION**, chopped
	1/2 cup **CELERY**, chopped
	2 cloves **GARLIC**, minced
	1 can (8 oz.) **TOMATO SAUCE**
	1 **BAY LEAF**
Several dashes of	**WORCESTERSHIRE SAUCE**
	TABASCO SAUCE
	SALT and **PEPPER**
	2 Tbsp. fresh **CILANTRO**, chopped (optional)

Cook 2 hours or until beans are tender. Serve in bowls with a garnish of **SOUR CREAM**, crumbled cooked **BACON** and chopped **GREEN ONIONS**.

Salads/Vegetables

RAGGED SOMBRERO

Quick, easy, delicious and colorful.

Cook until tender	2 **ONIONS**, chopped
	3 cloves **GARLIC**, minced
	1/4 cup **OIL**
Add and simmer 10 minutes	2 cans (10 oz. ea.) **CHOPPED TOMATOES** and **GREEN CHILIES**
	1 can (16 oz.) **TOMATOES**
	1 Tbsp. **CORIANDER**
	SALT and **PEPPER**
Dip one at a time in hot oil just to soften.............................	24 **CORN TORTILLAS**
Stack on paper towels and cut into one-fourths. Have grated	2 pounds **MONTEREY JACK CHEESE**

Layer tortillas, sauce and cheese in baking dish. To serve bake in preheated 350-degree oven 25 minutes or until hot. Serve **SOUR CREAM** on top.

HACIENDA SALAD

A layered salad, Southwest style.

For dressing mix together
and set aside .... 1 large ripe **AVOCADO,** mashed
$^1/_2$ cup **SOUR CREAM**
2 Tbsp. **ITALIAN DRESSING**
2 tsp. minced **ONION**
$^1/_2$ tsp. **CHILI POWDER**
$^1/_4$ tsp. **GARLIC SALT**

Toss together .... 2 cups **LETTUCE**, shredded
2 **TOMATOES**, chopped
2 Tbsp. minced **GREEN CHILIES**
$^1/_2$ cup **CHOPPED BLACK OLIVES**

Wash, drain and add .... 1 can (15 oz.) **CHILI BEANS**

Just before serving, layer salad mixture and dressing in large bowl. Top with **CHEDDAR CHEESE** and crushed **CORN CHIPS**. Serve with **PICANTE.**

SPANISH SUNSET AVOCADO SALAD

Quick, easy and delicious.

Mix together in jar .... $^1/_2$ cup **OLIVE OIL**
$^1/_4$ cup **WHITE WINE VINEGAR**
$^1/_4$ tsp. **PEPPER**
1 tsp. **GARLIC SALT**
2 Tbsp. **LEMON JUICE**

Cover tightly. Shake vigorously.
Combine in bowl .... 1 **AVOCADO**, chopped
1 **ONION**, chopped
1 **TOMATO**, chopped

Have shredded and set aside .... 1 **HEAD LETTUCE**

Pour dressing over bowl of vegetables and marinate in refrigerator for at least 30 minutes. Place lettuce on plate and spoon salad over it using a slotted spoon.

FIESTA BOWL
Actually an entree, disguised as a salad.

Brown in large skillet .... 1¹/₂ pounds **LEAN GROUND BEEF**
1 cup **GREEN PEPPER**, chopped
1¹/₂ cups **ONION**, chopped

Add .... 1 tsp. each **GARLIC SALT, CUMIN, SALT** and **PEPPER**
1 Tbsp. **CHILI POWDER**

Simmer 5 minutes. Set aside.
Prepare .... 1 head **LETTUCE,** shredded
2 **TOMATOES**, chopped
1 bag (6 oz.) **CORN CHIPS**, crush

Prepare **BASIC CON QUESO**. (Recipe in appetizers page 10.) In large glass salad bowl, layer in order, lettuce, tomatoes, chips, meat and hot cheese mixture. Serve with Con Queso on the side.

 HOT TIP

MEXICAN STAPLE: Wash and peel JICAMA. Slice into sticks. Sprinkle with CHILI POWDER.

▼ ▼ ▼ ▼ ▼ ▼ ▼ ▼ ▼ ▼ ▼ ▼ ▼ ▼ ▼ ▼ 93

LAYERED TEX-MEX CORNBREAD SALAD
Contrasting flavors and textures makes this dish interesting.

Mix and bake according to package directions. Then crumble	1 pkg. (6¹/₂ oz.) **CORNBREAD MIX**
Have the following ready.	
Open and drain	2 cans (15 oz. ea.) **PINTO BEANS**
Mix in separate bowl.................	2 cups **TOMATOES**, chopped
	1 cup **GREEN ONIONS**, chopped
	¹/₄ cup **JALAPENO PEPPERS**, seeded, chopped
Cook and crumble	12 slices **BACON**
Grate...	2 cups **MONTEREY JACK CHEESE**
Mix together in small bowl	1 cup **SOUR CREAM**
	1 cup **SALSA**

Layer half of each of the above in order listed. Repeat layering procedure with remaining ingredients in same order. Garnish with additional **SOUR CREAM** and **JALAPENO SLICES**. Cover and chill 2 to 3 hours before serving.

BAKED TORTILLA SHELLS
An edible salad bowl.

Wrap tortillas in foil. Place in preheated 350-degree oven for 10 minutes to soften. Lightly spray **TORTILLAS** on both sides with **COOKING SPRAY**. Press into oven-proof bowls to shape. One to each bowl. Bake for 15 minutes or until crisp.

CREAMY PICANTE DRESSING
This will wake up any salad.

Combine and mix well .... $^2/_3$ cup **MAYONNAISE**
$^1/_3$ cup **SOUR CREAM**
$^1/_2$ cup **PICANTE SAUCE**
$^1/_2$ tsp. **CUMIN**

Refrigerate and serve as a salad dressing.

FRIJOLES ESPECIAL
The "gourmet" version of a Southwest staple.

Clean and wash .... 3 cups **PINTO BEANS**

Cover with 6 cups **WATER** and soak overnight. Drain water and rinse. Add 4 cups **WATER**, bring to boil. Reduce heat and simmer 2 hours. Add following ingredients, chopped very fine: 1 **SWEET PEPPER**, 1 large **ONION**, 4 slices **BACON**, 1 can **TOMATOES** and **CHILIES**, 1 tablespoon **BROWN SUGAR**. **SALT** to taste. Cook 2 additional hours. (Add more water during cooking, if necessary.)

MIA AMIGAS VARIATION: Omit bacon. Add $1/4$ cup **MARGARINE** and 2 whole **FRESH BANANA PEPPERS**.

MIA AMIGOS VARIATION: Slice into $1/2$-inch pieces and boil for 10 minutes, 1 pound **GERMAN SAUSAGE**. Drain well. Add to beans last hour of cooking.

Refried beans may be prepared by using left over beans. Mash and fry in a little **BACON GREASE**. Continue mashing and stirring while cooking until dry and a little crusty.

HINT: Beans vary in cooking. Start early. May need more cooking. The longer they simmer, the more flavorful.

JALAPENO POTATOES
A new flavor for an old staple.

Cook until tender ....   4 medium **POTATOES**

Drain, peel and cut into ¼-inch slices. Set aside.

Melt in heavy saucepan ....   ¼ cup **MARGARINE**
Add and stir until smooth ....   1 Tbsp. **FLOUR**
Cook and stir for 1 minute.
   Gradually add ....   1 cup **MILK**
Cook until thickened. Add ....   1 roll (6 oz.) **JALAPENO CHEESE**

Stir until smooth. Layer in a greased casserole one-half of potatoes.

Top with one-half of ....   ½ cup chopped **GREEN PEPPER**
                                       1 jar (2 oz.) diced **PIMENTOS**

Repeat with remaining ingredients. Top with cheese sauce. Bake uncovered in pre-heated 350-degree oven for 40 minutes.

▼ ▼ ▼ ▼ ▼ ▼ ▼ ▼ ▼ ▼ ▼ ▼ ▼ ▼ ▼ ▼ ▼

MEXICAN CORN CASSEROLE
Serves 4 hungry GRINGOS or 6 average guests.

Mix together ....
1 can (16 oz.) **YELLOW CREAM-STYLE CORN**
1 cup **BISCUIT MIX**
1 **EGG**, beaten
2 Tbsp. **OIL**
$1/2$ cup **MILK**

Spread $1/2$ mixture in a greased 8x8x2-inch pan.

Cover with ....
1 can (4 oz.) **CHOPPED GREEN CHILIES**
6 ounces **MONTEREY JACK CHEESE**, grated
6 ounces **SHARP CHEDDAR CHEESE**, grated

Spread remaining corn mixture over top and bake in preheated 400-degree oven 30 minutes.

SPANISH RICE

A Mexican dinner would not be complete without this dish.

Place in skillet and brown ....
    1 cup **RICE**
    2 Tbsp. **OIL**
    1 **ONION,** chopped
    2 cloves **GARLIC,** minced

Chop and add ....
    1 can (16 oz.) **STEWED TOMATOES**
    1 can (14 oz.) **BEEF BROTH**
    SALT and **PEPPER**
    $1/2$ tsp. **CUMIN POWDER**

Cover and simmer 20 minutes or until tender and juice is absorbed.

 HOT TIP

COOKOUT . . . peel back shucks from ears of CORN. Remove silks. Brush with PICANTE. Replace shucks. Wrap in foil. Cook on grill.

▼ ▼ ▼ ▼ ▼ ▼ ▼ ▼ ▼ ▼ ▼ ▼ ▼ ▼ ▼ ▼ ▼ 99

NORMACITA'S MEXICAN SQUASH CASSEROLE

Cook until tender .... 1 pound **YELLOW SQUASH**, diced

Drain well. Add .... 4 Tbsp. **MARGARINE**
SALT and **PEPPER**

Set aside. Brown .... 1 pound **LEAN GROUND MEAT**
1 **ONION**, chopped

Remove from heat. Add 1 can (10 oz.) **CHOPPED CHILIES**
TOMATOES
1 can (8 oz.) **TOMATO SAUCE**
1 tsp. **CUMIN, OREGANO**
1 Tbsp. **CHILI POWDER**

Grate .... 3 cups **CHEESE**, any kind

Have ready to use .... 6 **CORN TORTILLAS**

Layer in buttered 9x13x2-inch baking dish, tortillas, squash, meat, cheese. Repeat, ending with cheese. Bake in preheated 350-degree oven 30 minutes.

GREEN CHILI CHEESE GRITS

A wonderful side dish with any entree, north or south of the border.

Cook according to directions .... 1 1/2 cup **GRITS**
Add .... 1 pound **SHARP CHEDDAR CHEESE**, grated
1/2 cup **MARGARINE**
3 tsp. **SEASONING SALT**
1 tsp. **PEPPER**
3 **EGGS**, slightly beaten
2 cans (4 oz. ea.) **CHOPPED GREEN CHILIES**, do not drain

Heat until cheese is melted. Pour into a buttered 9x13x2-inch baking dish. Bake in preheated 350-degree oven for 1 hour.

SUPER SPUDS . . . Top with SPICY TACO MEAT, CHEESE, RIPE OLIVES, PICANTE or SALSA. Create your own!!

BLACK BEAN DISH
May be used as a dip.

Heat in skillet	3 Tbsp. **MARGARINE**
Add and lightly brown	1 **ONION**, chopped
	2 cloves **GARLIC**, chopped
Add	2 cans (15 oz. ea.) **BLACK BEANS**
	1 **TOMATO**, chopped
	TABASCO, SALT and **PEPPER**
Add	$^1/_2$ cup each, grated **MEDIUM CHEDDAR,**
	SHARP CHEDDAR and **MONTEREY JACK**

Bake in preheated 350-degree oven for 30 minutes. Serve hot with **TORTILLA CHIPS**.

CHILI-POT BEANS. Brown 1 lb. GROUND BEEF and 1 chopped ONION. Add to cooked pot of BEANS. Season with 4 Tbsp. CHILI POWDER.

GORDITAS
Plump Tortillas

Mix in blender until smooth .....   1/2 tsp. crushed **RED PEPPER**
       1 can (8 oz.) **PINTO BEANS** with juice
       1 cup **WATER**
       1/2 tsp. **SALT**
Combine in separate bowl ....   1 3/4 cups **MASA HARINA**
       3/4 tsp. **SALT**
       1 tsp. **BAKING POWDER**

Add bean mixture, blend well. Cover, let stand 20 minutes. Divide into 24 portions. Pat into thin 2-inch rounds. Heat **OIL** in skillet. (Approximately 1/4-inch deep.) Fry, turning once, until crisp and brown. Drain on paper toweling. Top with **GUACAMOLE** and **SALSA**, or **PICA DE GALLO**. These are good sliced and filled with seasoned **MEAT MIXTURE**, **LETTUCE**, **TOMATOES**, and grated **CHEESE**. Serve as sandwiches with crisp **TORTILLA CHIPS**.

PAN DE MAIS

(Pahn deh mah-ees) Mexican cornbread with chilies and corn.

Mix with spoon ....
- 1 package (7 oz.) **MEXICAN JALAPENO CORNBREAD MIX**, dry
- 1 cup **SOUR CREAM**
- 1 can (15 oz.) **CREAM STYLE CORN**
- 1 can (4 oz.) **CHOPPED GREEN CHILIES**
- $1/2$ cup **OIL**
- 2 **EGGS**

Pour into a greased 9-inch baking dish. Bake in preheated 400-degree oven for 30 minutes or until set and slightly brown on top. Serve with **BUTTER** and **HONEY**. VARIATION: 1 cup grated **CHEDDAR CHEESE** and 1 tablespoon **INSTANT MINCED ONIONS** may be added.

INDIAN CORNBREAD: Mix CORNBREAD MIX according to directions. Pour on hot griddle size of pancakes. Sprinkle with mixture of grated CHEESE, chopped CHILIES drained, whole kernel CORN. Turn and brown.

Desserts

TRADITIONAL SOPAIPILLAS

Oh so yummy!

Mix together	2 cups **FLOUR**
	$1/2$ tsp. **SALT**
	$2^1/2$ tsp. **BAKING POWDER**
Cut in with pastry blender	2 Tbsp. **SHORTENING**
Add..	$3/4$ cup **WARM WATER**

Mix together and knead. Add more flour if necessary. Let stand 30 minutes. Roll on lightly floured board to $1/4$-inch thick. Cut into diamond shaped pieces with table knife. (Helps to seal them.) Fry in deep pan with 2 inches **OIL** at about 400-degrees. Drop in hot grease and turn at once so they will puff evenly on both sides. Brown slightly on both sides. These cook fast so cook only one at a time. Drain. Serve hot with **HONEY** and **BUTTER**, or dust with **CINNAMON** and **SUGAR**.

SOPAIPILLAS

Fried puffs.

Whip until almost stiff...............	1 cup **WHIPPING CREAM**
Add and beat	
1 minute longer.......................	1 Tbsp. **HONEY**
	2 Tbsp. **KAHLUA**
Sprinkle with..............................	**CINNAMON** or **NUTMEG**
Set aside.	
Cut into triangles....................	**FLOUR TORTILLAS**

Fry in **HOT OIL** (375-degrees) until lightly browned. Drain on paper towels. Cool. To serve, dip in whipped cream mixture.

TIRED or just LAZY??? Slightly thaw FROZEN YEAST ROLLS. Cut each roll in half. Drop in hot OIL. Fry until golden brown. Dust with POWDERED SUGAR or serve with HONEY.

▼ ▼ ▼ ▼ ▼ ▼ ▼ ▼ ▼ ▼ ▼ ▼ ▼ ▼ ▼ ▼ ▼

CAPIROTADA

Mexican bread pudding is traditionally served during Lent.

Split 5-count **BISCUITS** to make 10 biscuits. Cook according to directions on label. (May need to reduce cooking time slightly.) While biscuits are baking:

Beat with whisk	2 **EGGS**
Add	³/₄ cup **SUGAR**
	2 cups **MILK**
	¹/₂ tsp. **VANILLA**
	¹/₂ stick **MARGARINE**, melted
	RAISINS (optional)

Crumble biscuits into mixture. Stir slightly. Let stand 5 to 10 minutes. Pour into a buttered 8x8x2-inch baking dish. Bake in preheated 350-degree oven 30 minutes. Serve in individual dishes. Cover with GLAZE:

Simmer 10 minutes	2 cups **MILK**
	1 cup **SUGAR**
	1 Tbsp. each **FLOUR** and **BUTTER**
Remove from heat. Add	1 tsp. **VANILLA**

MEXICAN COBBLER
Good and very pretty.

Mix together and
heat to boiling .... 1 to 1¹/₂ cups **SUGAR**
1 package frozen **FRUIT**
¹/₂ cup **WATER**

Set aside.

Melt **BUTTER** in small skillet. Soften 8 to 10 **FLOUR TORTILLAS** in butter by turning once and placing on plate. Using slotted spoon, place fruit in middle of tortilla. Roll like enchilada, place seam down in oblong casserole dish. Pour remaining juice over tortillas, sprinkle with **SUGAR.** Let set for 30 minutes. (If cobbler looks too dry, add more liquid, **WATER** or **JUICE**.) Bake 20 to 25 minutes in preheated 350-degree oven. May serve with **ICE CREAM** or **COOL WHIP**.

TORTILLA FRUIT ROLLUPS
The perfect ending to a Mexican dinner!

Open and set aside .... 1 can (21 oz.) **STRAWBERRY FRUIT PIE FILLING**

Prepare 8 to 10 **FLOUR TORTILLAS**. (Soften in butter in small skillet, or heat in microwave, if not fresh enough to roll.) Place fruit filling in middle of each tortilla and roll like an enchilada. Place seam down in 13x9x2-inch baking dish.

Mix together in saucepan .... 2 cups **WATER**
1¹/₂ cups **SUGAR**
³/₄ cup **MARGARINE**

Bring to a boil. Add .... 1 tsp. **ALMOND FLAVORING**

Pour mixture over filled tortillas. Place in refrigerator and let soak 1 to 24 hours. Baste with sugar mixture before and during baking. Bake in a preheated 350-degree oven for 20 to 25 minutes or until hot and slightly browned. Extra special touch!! Serve with **ICE CREAM**!! VARIATION: use any **FRUIT PIE FILLING** you prefer.

BIZCOCHITOS

A crusty sweet biscuit. Great with chocolate or coffee.

Cream together.............................. 1/2 cup **BUTTER**
2 Tbsp. **POWDERED SUGAR**

Add.. 1 cup, less 2 Tbsp., **FLOUR**
1 cup **PECANS**, chopped
1 tsp. **VANILLA**

Roll dough into 1-inch balls. Place on a greased baking sheet. Flatten with bottom of a glass that has been dipped in **POWDERED SUGAR**. Bake in a preheated 300-degree oven for 15 to 20 minutes. When done, roll in powdered sugar while still warm.

SWEET TOOTH — Butter a FLOUR TORTILLA, sprinkle with CIN-NAMON and SUGAR. Fold over and place in oven or microwave until warm.

▼ ▼ ▼ ▼ ▼ ▼ ▼ ▼ ▼ ▼ ▼ ▼ ▼ ▼ ▼ ▼ ▼ 111

ICE CREAM FILLED CINNAMON TORTILLAS
OH-SO GOOD!!!

Mix and set aside .... ⅓ cup **SUGAR**
2 tsp. **GROUND CINNAMON**

Pour oil (3-inches deep) into saucepan that is 1½-inches <u>smaller</u> around than the **FLOUR TORTILLAS**. Fry tortillas, one at a time. Hold bottom in oil with metal ladle to make bowl shape. (May use a canning jar.) Fry to light brown. Drain on paper towels. While warm, sprinkle with sugar/cinnamon mixture. To serve: Fill with scoop of **VANILLA ICE CREAM**. Spoon **KAHLUA** over ice cream.

IMPRESSIVE! Melt ½ cup CHOCOLATE CHIPS and 1 tsp. OIL in microwave. Paint inside of 6 CRISP TORTILLA BOWLS. Refrigerate. Blend until smooth, 1 can drained APRICOT HALVES with 2 Tbsp. HONEY. Mix with 3 cups fresh or canned FRUIT. Spoon into shells. Top with COOL WHIP.

BUNUELOS

Light, crispy Mexican fritters are a New Year's tradition.

In large bowl mix .... 3 cups **FLOUR**, sifted
1 tsp. **BAKING POWDER**
1 tsp. **SALT**
2 Tbsp. **SUGAR**
Cut into mixture .... $^1/_2$ cup **MARGARINE**, softened
Add and mix well .... 2 **EGGS**
$^3/_4$ cup **MILK**

Knead until very smooth. Shape into 20 balls. Cover and let stand 30 minutes. Heat **OIL** 2-inches deep in large saucepan or deep fryer. Roll each ball out on a lightly floured surface into very thin 6-inch circles. Fry only 1 at a time until golden brown, turning once. Drain on paper towels. Sprinkle with mixture of 1 cup **SUGAR** and 1 teaspoon **CINNAMON**.

COYOTE DRIPPINGS

Praline covered cheese puffs. Very addictive!

Place in large roaster,
   set aside .... 22 ounces **CHEESE PUFFS**
Combine and boil 5 minutes ..... 2 cups **BROWN SUGAR**
                              1 cup **MARGARINE**
                              $^1/_2$ cup **DARK CORN SYRUP**
Remove from heat. Add .... $^1/_2$ tsp. **SODA**

Pour over cheese puffs and stir coating well. Bake in a preheated 250-degree oven for 1 hour. Stir every 10 to 15 minutes while baking to coat evenly. Dump out on wax paper and separate. Cool. ENJOY!

YUMMY SPREAD: Blend equal parts HONEY and BUTTER or MAR-GARINE. Great on SOPIAPILLAS, BREAD, etc. (May substitute FRUIT JAMS for honey.)

"MEXICO CITY" EARTHQUAKE CAKE

Finished cake will have cracks and crevices.

Spray 9x13x2-inch baking pan with non-stick spray.

Layer in prepared pan ....   1 cup **COCONUT**
                                           1 cup chopped **PECANS**

Prepare according
  to directions ....   1 **GERMAN CHOCOLATE CAKE MIX**

Pour over coconut and nut mixture.

Mix well....................................... $^1/_2$ cup **MARGARINE**, softened
                                           8 ounces **CREAM CHEESE**
                                           1 tsp. **VANILLA**
                                           16 ounces **POWDERED SUGAR**

Spoon over cake batter. Bake in preheated 350-degree oven for 40 to 50 minutes.

MEXICAN FRUIT CAKE
So delicious! There is never any left.

Beat well	2 **EGGS**
Add and beat until fluffy	2 cups **SUGAR**
Add	2 tsp. **BAKING SODA**
	2 cups **FLOUR**
	1 can (20 oz.) **CRUSHED PINEAPPLE**, do not drain
	1 cup **PECANS**, chopped

Mix well. Pour into a greased and floured 9x13x2-inch baking dish. Bake in pre-heated 350-degree oven 30 to 35 minutes. Completely cool cake.

Top with **CREAM CHEESE FROSTING**:

Cream until fluffy	6 ounces **CREAM CHEESE**, softened
Add	2 cups **CONFECTIONER'S SUGAR**
	1/4 cup **MARGARINE**, softened
	1 tsp. **VANILLA**

KAHLUA CAKE
This gets first-class results every time.

Beat together .... 1 **YELLOW CAKE MIX** (no pudding)
1 box (8 oz.) **INSTANT CHOCOLATE PUDDING**
$^3/_4$ cup **OIL**
$^3/_4$ cup **WATER**
$^1/_2$ cup **SUGAR**

Add one at a time .... 4 **EGGS**

Add.. $^1/_4$ cup **KAHLUA**
$^1/_4$ cup **VODKA**

Blend together and pour in slightly greased bundt pan. Bake in preheated 350-degree oven for 1 hour or until toothpick inserted comes out clean. Punch holes in hot cake and pour mixture of $^1/_4$ cup **KAHLUA** and $^1/_4$ cup **POWDERED SUGAR**. Cool in pan. Invert to serving dish.

AMARETTO CUSTARD
Topped off with chocolate sauce. U-M-M-M!

Beat well	3 **EGGS**
Add and set aside	4 Tbsp. **SUGAR**
	1 tsp. **VANILLA**
	1/4 cup **AMARETTO**
	Dash of **SALT**
Add	1 1/4 cups **MILK**

Pour mixture into 4 custard cups. Place in circle in microwave oven. Cook at medium (50% power) for 6 to 10 minutes or until almost set in the center. Rearrange cups every 2 minutes. Chill thoroughly. Heat **CHOCOLATE SYRUP** according to directions on container. Invert custard onto serving plates, spoon chocolate syrup over custard. Top with sliced **ALMONDS**.

IT'S QUICK — IT'S GOOD! Pour KAHLUA or AMARETTO over ICE CREAM for quick dessert. Check page 284 in MORE CALF FRIES to CAVIAR to make your own liquers. Fun Christmas gifts.

PUMPKIN FLAN

This is very good. One of the best flans we have tasted.

Place in heavy skillet .... $^3/_4$ cup **SUGAR**

Cook, stirring constantly until deep golden brown. Immediately pour into an 8x8-inch oven-proof dish. Rotate dish until syrup covers bottom.

Beat together .... 1 cup **CANNED PUMPKIN**
$^3/_4$ cup **SUGAR**
1 tsp. **GROUND CINNAMON**
$^1/_4$ tsp. each **GINGER, ALLSPICE, NUTMEG**
6 **EGGS**

Beat well. Add .... 1 cup **HALF** and **HALF CREAM**
1 cup **WHIPPING CREAM**
$^1/_2$ tsp. **VANILLA**

Pour over syrup. Place dish in a larger roasting pan. Pour **HOT WATER** into bottom pan 1-inch deep. Bake in preheated 350-degree oven 1 to $1^1/_4$ hours or until knife inserted in center comes clean. Remove from water. Cool. Refrigerate. Loosen side of flan with knife; unmold. Keep refrigerated.

COCONUT FLAN
Good 'cross any border!!!

Melt in heavy skillet .... 1 cup **SUGAR**

Stir constantly until it becomes a deep amber syrup. Pour into well chilled, **BUTTERED** dish. Turn to coat bottom. Set aside.

Beat well .... 7 **EGGS**

Add .... 1 quart **HALF N' HALF**

1 can (15 oz.) **CREAM OF COCONUT**

$^1/_2$ cup **SUGAR**

Pour over caramelized sugar. Set baking dish in pan of **HOT WATER**. Bake in preheated 325-degree oven 1 hour or until set. Chill and invert onto serving dish. Garnish with **CHOCOLATE SAUCE**.

MEXICAN FLAN

A popular Mexican dessert.

Beat until well blended	8 **EGGS**
Add	$^2/_3$ cup **SUGAR**
	$^1/_4$ tsp. **SALT**
Beat in	$3^1/_2$ cups **EVAPORATED MILK**
	2 tsp. **VANILLA**

Sprinkle $^1/_2$ cup **LIGHT BROWN SUGAR** on the bottom of an 8x8-inch oven-proof baking dish; gently pour custard mixture over brown sugar. Place baking dish into larger pan. Add hot water to bottom pan. (Approximately 1-inch deep.) Bake in preheated 350-degree oven for 1 hour or until knife inserted comes out clean. Refrigerate overnight. Before serving, run knife around edge of pan and turn out onto small platter.

To enhance this dessert's flavor, cover with thin layer of **LIGHT BROWN SUGAR** after refrigerating overnight, place under broiler and lightly brown immediately before serving.

CARAMEL CHEESECAKE FLAN
The marriage of two favorite desserts.

Melt in small skillet,
   stirring occasionally .... 1 cup **SUGAR**

Pour into ungreased, 2-quart baking dish. Tilt to coat bottom and sides.

Combine in large mixer .... 2 packages (8 oz. ea.) **CREAM CHEESE**
                                  1 can (14 oz.) **SWEETENED CONDENSED MILK**
                                  4 **EGGS**

Pour into caramel coated dish. Place flan in larger baking pan and fill halfway up sides with **HOT WATER**. Bake in preheated 325-degree oven for approximately 1 hour and 15 minutes, or until knife inserted in center comes out clean. Remove from water and place on a rack to cool. Completely chill in refrigerator. To unmold; loosen outer edges of flan with a thin knife, place serving plate over flan and invert. Scrape additional sauce from mold and spoon over. To serve; garnish with **WHIPPED CREAM** and **TOASTED ALMONDS**.

PECAN PRALINES
A soft, creamy praline. Muy bueno!

Mix well..
1 pound **LIGHT BROWN SUGAR**
8 ounces **SOUR CREAM**
3 Tbsp. **WHITE CORN SYRUP**
$1/4$ tsp. **SODA**

Let set overnight in refrigerator. Cook real slow to soft ball stage. (235 degrees on candy thermometer.) Add 2 cups coarsely cut up **PECANS**. Beat until almost ready to set. Place by teaspoonfuls on wax paper that has been lightly sprinkled with **SALT**.

LIGHT after HEAVY meal!! Combine 12 oz. LIGHT WHIPPED TOP-PING, $1/2$ cup SUGAR, 1 cup BUTTERMILK, 3 chopped BANANAS, NUTS. Freeze.

▼ ▼ ▼ ▼ ▼ ▼ ▼ ▼ ▼ ▼ ▼ ▼ ▼ ▼ ▼ ▼ ▼

MICROWAVE PECAN-PEANUT BRITTLE
Excellent with Mexican food when made with pecans.

Mix in microwave
proof dish ....
- 1 cup **PECANS** or **RAW PEANUTS**
- 1 cup **SUGAR**
- $1/2$ cup **WHITE KARO**

Cook on HIGH for 7 to 8 minutes. Stir once.

Add...
- 1 tsp. **MARGARINE**
- 1 tsp. **VANILLA**

Microwave 2 more minutes.
Remove and add ....
- 1 tsp. **SODA**

Stir until foamy. Pour onto a buttered cookie sheet. When cool, break into pieces. Store in airtight container.

INDEX

▼ ▼ ▼ ▼ ▼ ▼ ▼ ▼ ▼ ▼ ▼ ▼ ▼ ▼ ▼ ▼ ▼

Jan-Su Publications
1012 North 9th, Lamesa, Texas 79331, Phone 806-872-8667

Please send me _____ copies of **Calf Fries to Caviar**	@ 14.95	_____
Postage and handling (per book)	@ 2.50	_____
Please send me _____ copies of **More Calf Fries to Caviar**	@ 14.95	_____
Postage and handling (per book)	@ 2.50	_____
Please send me _____ copies of **'Cross the Border**	@ 8.95	_____
Postage and handling (per book)	@ 2.00	_____
Texas residents add appropriate sales tax		_____
Gift Wrap (per book)	@ 2.50	_____
	Total	_____

Name _____

Address _____

City, State, Zip _____

Make check payable to ***Jan-Su Publications*** • No C.O.D.'s
Prices subject to change • We accept Credit Card orders

- -

Jan-Su Publications
1012 North 9th, Lamesa, Texas 79331, Phone 806-872-8667

Please send me _____ copies of **Calf Fries to Caviar**	@ 14.95	_____
Postage and handling (per book)	@ 2.50	_____
Please send me _____ copies of **More Calf Fries to Caviar**	@ 14.95	_____
Postage and handling (per book)	@ 2.50	_____
Please send me _____ copies of **'Cross the Border**	@ 8.95	
Postage and handling (per book)	@ 2.00	_____
Texas residents add appropriate sales tax		_____
Gift Wrap (per book)	@ 2.50	_____
	Total	_____

Name _____

Address _____

City, State, Zip _____

Make check payable to *Jan-Su Publications* • No C.O.D.'s
Prices subject to change • We accept Credit Card orders

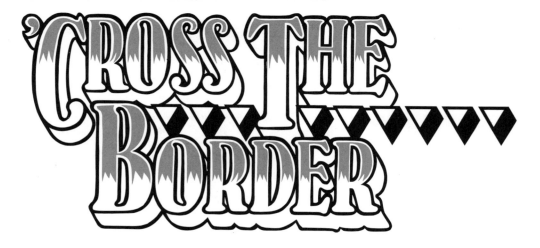

Southwest Cuisine

by Janel Franklin and Sue Vaughn

Publishers of **CALF FRIES to CAVIAR** and **MORE CALF FRIES to CAVIAR**

Copyright ©1993 by JAN-SU PUBLICATIONS
All rights reserved
ISBN 0-9610956-2-8

Additional copies may be obtained at the cost of $8.95 per book,
plus $2.00 postage and handling. Texas residents add appropriate, tax.
JAN-SU PUBLICATIONS
1012 North 9th, Lamesa, Texas 79331, 806-872-8667

First Printing   1993
Second Printing   1996

Printed in the USA by

WIMMER
The Wimmer Companies, Inc.
Memphis

'CROSS THE BORDER is a Fiesta: A celebration of color, fun, and the most sizzling, zesty, taste-tempting Southwestern recipes available. Like CALF FRIES TO CAVIAR and MORE CALF FRIES TO CAVIAR, we added our special touch — easy to find ingredients, simple to follow instructions, short on cooking methods, but always long on flavor! We hope you enjoy our favorites!

Janel & Sue

▼ ▼

Table of Contents